Animals
That Live in the
Forest

Deer

by JoAnn Early Macken

Reading consultant: Susan Nations, M.Ed., author/literacy coach/consultant

W R WEEKLY READER
EARLY LEARNING LIBRARY

Please visit our web site at: www.earlyliteracy.cc
For a free color catalog describing Weekly Reader® Early Learning Library's list
of high-quality books, call 1-877-445-5824 (USA) or 1-800-387-3178 (Canada).
Weekly Reader® Early Learning Library's fax: (414) 336-0164.

Library of Congress Cataloging-in-Publication Data

Macken, JoAnn Early, 1953–
    Deer / JoAnn Early Macken.
       p. cm. — (Animals that live in the forest)
    Includes bibliographical references and index.
    ISBN 0-8368-4481-5 (lib. bdg.)
    ISBN 0-8368-4488-2 (softcover)
    1. Deer—Juvenile literature. I. Title.
  QL737.U55M25   2005
  599.65—dc22   2004057200

This edition first published in 2005 by
Weekly Reader® Early Learning Library
330 West Olive Street, Suite 100
Milwaukee, WI 53212 USA

Art direction: Tammy West
Cover design and page layout: Kami Koenig
Picture research: Diane Laska-Swanke

Picture credits: Cover, pp. 5, 13, 19 © Tom and Pat Leeson; p. 7 © Alan &
Sandy Carey; pp. 9, 15, 21 © Michael H. Francis; p. 11 © Dave Welling;
p. 17 © Arthur Morris/Visuals Unlimited

Printed in the United States of America

1 2 3 4 5 6 7 8 9 09 08 07 06 05

Note to Educators and Parents

Reading is such an exciting adventure for young children! They are beginning to integrate their oral language skills with written language. To encourage children along the path to early literacy, books must be colorful, engaging, and interesting; they should invite the young reader to explore both the print and the pictures.

Animals That Live in the Forest is a new series designed to help children read about forest creatures. Each book describes a different forest animal's life cycle, eating habits, home, and behavior.

Each book is specially designed to support the young reader in the reading process. The familiar topics are appealing to young children and invite them to read — and re-read — again and again. The full-color photographs and enhanced text further support the student during the reading process.

In addition to serving as wonderful picture books in schools, libraries, homes, and other places where children learn to love reading, these books are specifically intended to be read within an instructional guided reading group. This small group setting allows beginning readers to work with a fluent adult model as they make meaning from the text. After children develop fluency with the text and content, the book can be read independently. Children and adults alike will find these books supportive, engaging, and fun!

— Susan Nations, M.Ed., author, literacy coach,
and consultant in literacy development

In the shade of a tree, a **fawn** lies still. Only its mother knows the baby deer is there. Its spots help it hide. They look like spots of sunlight on the grass.

4

5

The female deer, or **doe**, comes to feed the fawn. For its first few months, the fawn drinks milk from its mother. When it is a few days old, it starts to eat plants, too.

After a few weeks, the fawn walks with its mother. After a few months, the fawn's coat changes. It loses its white spots. Deer's coats are reddish brown in summer. In winter, they are gray.

Young deer play, kick, and leap. They chase each other. Male deer, or **bucks**, grow antlers each year. The antlers fall off in winter.

11

In spring and summer, deer eat leaves and berries. In fall, they eat acorns and grass. In winter, they eat bark and twigs.

Deer are good swimmers. They often wade into lakes to get away from insects that bite.

15

Deer can see all around them. They can see things that move. They swivel their ears to hear better. They watch and listen for danger.

If a deer finds danger, it may snort. It may stomp its feet on the ground. Deer can leap high in the air. When they run, their white tails flash a warning.

At night, they rest in safe places. Most deer beds have plants around them. Deer are at home in the forest.

Glossary

antlers — bony growths on an animal's head

fawn — a baby deer

snort — to make a noise by blowing air out through the nose

stomp — to pound with the bottom of the foot

swivel — to turn

For More Information

Books

All About Deer. Jim Arnosky (Scholastic)

Deer. Busy Baby Animals (series). Jinny Johnson
(Gareth Stevens)

Deer: Graceful Grazers. The Wild World
of Animals (series). Jody Sullivan (Capstone)

Fawn to Deer. Animals Growing Up (series).
Jason Cooper (Rourke)

Web Sites

Natureworks
www.nhptv.org/natureworks/whitetaileddeer.htm
Pictures and information about white-tailed deer

23

Index

About the Author

JoAnn Early Macken is the author of two rhyming picture books, *Sing-Along Song* and *Cats on Judy*, and six other series of nonfiction books for beginning readers. Her poems have appeared in several children's magazines. A graduate of the M.F.A. in Writing for Children and Young Adults program at Vermont College, she lives in Wisconsin with her husband and their two sons. Visit her Web site at www.joannmacken.com.